Soaring with Eagles

BILL NEWMAN

**BILL
NEWMAN
INTERNATIONAL**

Published by
BILL NEWMAN INTERNATIONAL
P.O. BOX 195
TOOWONG, QLD 4066
Australia
Tel (07) 371 0750, Fax (07) 8701664

FOREWORD

I have always been fascinated with eagles, one of God's most interesting and impressive creatures. Anyone who has spent much time around me knows this. The coach Birdie and I own has eagles painted on the side. I have spoken about eagles often from the stage. Over the years I have given and received sculptures, drawings and paintings of "the king of birds". I simply like these awesome birds.

Perhaps the reason I love eagles so much is the character traits they represent. They seem so fearless, bold and full of strength - qualities that I admire. Above all they symbolize true freedom as they glide through the heavens. Who can see an eagle in flight, even in films or pictures, and not be stirred deeply?

There aren't many books that have impressed me as much as Dr Bill Newman's *The Power of a Successful Life*. So it is especially exciting now that Bill has written an entire book about my favorite birds, capturing their spirit and majesty in *Soaring with Eagles*. Best of all, Bill has used what he calls "the monarchs of the skies" to teach us powerful principles about life, success and achievement.

With such chapter titles as, "From the Nest to Maturity", "Soaring Above the Winds of Adversity" and "Living Like an Eagle", Bill relates truth after truth about using our God-given talents and abilities to make a difference in our world.

In the first chapter he relates the story of a butterfly struggling to free itself from a cocoon and a sympathetic traveller who cut it loose. The butterfly was released, but all the brilliant coloring - which would have appeared as the struggling continued - was gone. Bill then hits the reader with this note - "Great trials are often necessary to prepare us for great responsibilities." These things aren't always what a person likes to read or hear, but they can free you to take charge of your life and to understand why challenges happen.

Throughout the book he continues to explain truth after truth, spotlighting lots of stories in each chapter. For example, I had heard about the two sets of an eagle's eyelids before, but I never understood as much about the importance of these eyelids until I read Chapter five. What a great lesson in developing, protecting and "firing" (as Bill calls it) your vision!

I especially like the final chapter, "Come Fly", in which he writes, "It's time to give up your small ambitions. It's time to take a leap like the eagle, to stretch those wings, to rise above the mountains, through the clouds."

I hope I have whetted your appetite, because I know you are going to enjoy this book, page after powerful page. You can read it at one sitting, plus you can go back, time after time, to re-discover the lessons you may have overlooked before.

If you want to become a great achiever here's the book to help you make it happen. You <u>can</u> succeed and Bill Newman has provided the flight pattern. Here's the book that will give you the courage to start *Soaring with Eagles!*

- Dexter R Yager, Sr.

Contents

THIS BOOK CAN CHANGE YOUR LIFE!

Often when reading a book we decide to apply what we read to our lives. All too often, weeks later, we have forgotten our good intentions. Here are 5 practical ways of:-

TURNING GOOD INTENTIONS INTO PRACTICAL HABITS

1. USE CARDS

Write out the principles or passages you want to memorise on 3" x 5" cards and review them often.

2. MARK YOUR CALENDAR

Mark your calendar daily for the time when you will review your good intentions.

3. RE-READ YOUR UNDERLINES

Underline key portions of this book, then re-read your underlines over and over.

4. APPLY THE MATERIAL IMMEDIATELY

There is an old saying:
>   Hear something - you forget it,
>   See something - you remember it, and
>   Do something - you understand it.

Apply what you learn as soon as you possibly can - it helps you understand and remember it.

5. PRIORITISE WHAT YOU WANT TO LEARN

Select 1-3 things from the book, apply them faithfully and make them a habit. Remember, every person alive struggles with turning their good intentions into habits. Using these 5 points will turn wishing into doing.

Introduction

INTRODUCTION

Eagles are magnificent creatures. We were driving as a family in the mountains and as we rounded a bend there was a huge wedge-tailed eagle. He wasn't flustered but just hopped to the edge of the cliff, jumped into the air, put out his beautiful wings and soared off down into the valley below.

The eagle is one of the largest and most powerful birds in the world. Eagles rank second in size only to the Californian condor among birds of prey in North America. At close range eagles look fierce and proud. As a result they are pictured as fierce, courageous hunters. Some eagles gracefully soar high in the air hunting for food. Because of this eagles have long been symbols of freedom and power. The *golden eagle* best fits both of these descriptions and is sometimes called, "king of birds".

The eagle, for its size, is the most powerful and feared bird alive. In Australia they can knock kangaroos and small sheep from cliff tops. With boldness and courage they attack animals much larger than themselves. There are about 8,500 species of birds in the world, but there are only about 60 species of eagles. They are the king of the birds, the symbol of the conqueror. Roman warriors used a golden figure of an eagle as a sign of strength and bravery. Russian and Austrian emperors also used eagles as symbols. The United States chose the bald eagle as its national bird in 1782.

Golden and bald eagles are from 76-89 centimetres (30-35 inches) long from the bill to the tip of the tail. They weigh from 3.6-6 kilograms (8-13 pounds). They have a wingspread of about 2 metres (7 feet). Other eagles are much smaller. For example the *hawk eagles* of Africa and Asia are only 46-56 centimetres (18-22 inches) long. Female eagles are slightly larger than males. Golden eagles are strong. When the wind is especially favourable golden eagles are believed able to carry prey weighing as much as their own weight to their nest.

CHARACTERISTICS OF EAGLES

There is their speed, strength, power, majesty, their boldness, dependability, courage, tenderness, faithfulness, pride, ferocity and great daring which give them the dominion of the skies.

In these next few pages let us allow the monarch of the skies, the eagle, to teach us how our lives can count.

If you think you are beaten, you are.
If you think you dare not, you don't.
If you like to win, but you think you can't,
It is almost certain you won't.

If you think you'll lose, you're lost.
For out of the world we find
Success begins with a person's will -
It's all in the state of the mind.

If you think you're outclassed, you are.
You've got to think high to rise,
You've got to be sure of yourself before
You can ever win a prize.

Life's battles don't always go
To the stronger woman or man,
But sooner or later the one who wins
Is the one WHO THINKS, "I CAN!"

Life responds to our expectations.

It's time to fly.

It's time to soar with the eagles.

> **Chapter**
> # 1

From The Nest To Maturity

1. FROM THE NEST TO MATURITY

Unborn Eagle

Before an eagle is even born, they actually have a small tooth on their beak and that helps them to break out of the egg. If anyone tries to help that eagle chick to escape, it will probably not survive because breaking through the egg is the tenacity and the fight that the eagle needs to make it in life. It is one thing to itch for something and another thing to scratch for it!

<u>KEEP CLIMBING</u>

Life is a struggle, a continual climb, if we're ever to reach our goal;
For the road of life is rough and rugged, with many a stone in the way;

And only with courage and a will to win can we reach the summit one day.

The higher you climb, the better the view - keep right on going, never say stop;
Keep on pushing your way to the top.
There will be many on the road of life to caution you of the dangers you face,
Suggesting you turn back, give up the goal, and with them your footsteps retrace.
Right then is the time to show your courage and decide for once and for all
That your life's task lies directly ahead and on this decision rise or fall;
Then push on to the heights sublime, not back to the land of ease.

A traveller in Africa saw one of the large butterflies of the tropics struggling to free itself from the cocoon. He pitied it and, with his knife, cut the cords at which it was straining. It was released but all the brilliant colouring was gone! The struggle was necessary to make the colour appear. As you gain the victory over trial and adversity you will see beautiful colours and qualities come from your life. People who have never had difficulties or problems tend to be very shallow.

Great trials are often necessary to prepare us for great responsibilities. The longer you dwell on your misfortunes, the greater is their power to control you. No diamond or gem has ever been polished without friction. It is the irritation in the oyster that produces the pearl. The problems, difficulties and setbacks we have in life are all required for our development.

Sir Winston Churchill, during one of his many visits to his old school at Harrow, addressed the students in the following way:

He was in the big dining hall that affords a view of the lights of London from Harrow on the Hill. The headmaster introduced the five foot five, 235 pound intellectual giant in a flourishing manner. After graciously acknowledging the profuse introduction, Churchill made that never-to-be-forgotten statement, "Young gentlemen, never give up, never give up, never give up, never, never, never, never." Then he sat down.

There is no mistake as great as the mistake of not going on.

It is always too soon to quit. I don't know what mountain you have to climb, what the burden is you have to carry, what problems you are facing, what trials and difficulties are surrounding you. But I know this - it is too soon to quit - never give up.

Success consists of getting up just one more time than you fall. It is like the postage stamp - its usefulness consists in the ability to stick to one thing until it gets there.

On his voyage to discover America, as day after day no land appeared and again and again his sailors threatened mutiny and tried to persuade him to turn back, Columbus refused to listen to their entreaties and entered each day in the ship's log-book the two words, "Sailed on!"

The greatest failure in life is to stop trying.

Maybe you have tried to get a job many times. Get up, brush the dust off and go again. Perhaps your business is down, stand back and review and go again.

It is always too soon to quit. Never give up. Persist.

Men do not <u>fail</u>. They just give up easily.

The tougher the job, the greater the reward. No one can cheat you out of ultimate success but yourself.

Perhaps it is time for you to leave the comfort zone of the egg. Sure, breaking through the shell is tough and life outside is going to be tougher, but life - with all its excitement and rewards - lies ahead.

<u>WHAT IS LIFE?</u>

Life is a challenge	- *meet it*
Life is a gift	- *accept it*
Life is an adventure	- *dare it*
Life is a sorrow	- *overcome it*

Life is a tragedy	- *face it*
Life is a duty	- *perform it*
Life is a game	- *play it*
Life is a mystery	- *unfold it*
Life is a song	- *sing it*
Life is an opportunity	- *take it*
Life is a journey	- *complete it*
Life is a promise	- *fulfil it*
Life is a beauty	- *praise it*
Life is a struggle	- *fight it*
Life is a goal	- *achieve it*
Life is a puzzle	- *solve it*

Life is like a taxi - the meter just keeps on ticking whether you are getting somewhere or just standing still! The vast majority of people let life pass them by, just too afraid to extend themselves. I love to watch a little baby fight and struggle to crawl, to stand, to walk, to talk. It is tragic to see the fight lost as they grow older. To seize life is going to require effort, to do more than expected.

DO MORE

Do more than exist	- *live*
Do more than touch	- *feel*
Do more than look	- *observe*
Do more than read	- *absorb*
Do more than hear	- *listen*
Do more than listen	- *understand*
Do more than think	- *ponder*

Do more than plan   *- act*
Do more than talk   *- say something*

You will never discover your full potential if you stay in the comfort zone. Break out - the world is waiting.

Learning to Fly

While the eaglet is still in the nest it begins hopping from rim to rim. Later it stretches its wings and flaps them awkwardly. Finally the hopping turns to jumping. Some jumps are as high as fifteen feet above the nest. The result of all this preparation is that the eaglet's first flight is almost always successful and may extend for a mile or more.

Most eagles voluntarily fly from the nest between their tenth and fifteenth week. However if a reluctant eaglet decides to stay in the nest, its parents may withhold food. Rather than bringing dinner to the nest, the parents leave it on a nearby limb. Eventually hunger motivates the eaglet to take its first flight.

The eagles spend a lot of time just teaching their young to fly. The mother eagle and the father eagle are demonstrating to their young all the time how to fly. They will keep pushing them. They will even push them out of the nest and will fly down and pick them up again and take them away on their wings (carried away on the wings of eagles). Then if the young are still not getting out of the nest and things are a little bit too comfortable, the eagle will (even before building the nest they put sharp stones and even thorns into the nest and cover them over with wool and feathers to make it comfortable) start pulling out the bits of wool and feathers just to make it uncomfortable in that nest.

It's great. You have decided to break out of the shell and leave the comfort zone. Now it's time to learn to fly. You look over the edge. Help! I can't do it. It's too high. I've never done anything like this before!

> It's time to make the jump,
> It's time to say "yes" to life,
> It's time to give up your small ambitions.

You will never reach some distant shore if you are afraid to leave the safety of the harbour.

Get those wings going. They can lift you. Perseverance will help you overcome almost any obstacle. Stop making excuses for yourself. It is time, there is no gain without pain.

Art Linkletter tells the following story of Wendy Stoker, a young 19 year old from Cedar Rapids, Iowa, who was studying at the University of Florida:-

Last year she was placed third, just 2 1/2 points from first, in the Iowa girls' state diving championships. She'd worked two hours a day for four years to get there.

Now at the University of Florida she's working twice as hard and has earned the number two position on the varsity diving team and she's aiming for the national finals. Wendy is carrying a full academic load, finds time for bowling and is an accomplished water-skier.

*But perhaps the most remarkable thing about Wendy Stoker is her typing. She bangs out forty-five words a minute on her typewriter - **with her toes**.*

Oh, did I fail to mention? Wendy was born without arms.

Are you prepared to master your own weakness? The three greatest words in the English language for fulfilment are - DO IT NOW. Don't wait. DO IT NOW.

The gain is worth the pain.

Start now with a list of valuable objectives.

• Having a happier marriage

• Being more open and understanding with your children

• Creating more family times together

• Losing weight and getting back into condition

- Travel

- Attending classes at the local college

- Learning to play a new sport

- Becoming an extended family to children or young people who have no parents or grandparents.

- Building that business

Let your thoughts run free and think of others. Ultimately we become the people we choose to be. Although we live together, each of us grows alone.

Seize life before life seizes you. Even if you are on the right track, you will get run over if you just sit there! If the eagle chick does not break out of the shell it is going to get pretty smelly and hot in there anyway.

I bargained with Life for a penny,
And Life would pay no more
However I begged at evening
When I counted my scanty store.

For Life is a just employer,
He gives you what you ask;
But once you have set the wages,
Why, you must bear the task.

I worked for a menial's hire,
Only to learn, dismayed,
That any wage I had asked of Life
Life would have willingly paid.
[Poet Unknown]

Don't waste your life for mere pennies. Are you prepared to commit the courage and discipline necessary to make your dreams come true? If not you are missing the greatest thrill of all.

Commit yourself to something great and wonderful - something bigger than yourself.

If you do it will change your life.

Make the jump - fly.

Wind Beneath Your Wings

2. WIND BENEATH YOUR WINGS

Soaring

The eagle is an aerodynamic marvel, a perfect flying machine, well able to maintain flight for lengthy periods without undue exertion. In fact it can remain completely motionless except for an occasional flip of the wing tips to counter wind currents.

Eagles soar higher than practically any other bird alive; they understand the ways of the thermal currents better than most, if not all birds. Their soaring takes them so high they are barely visible to the naked eye. Airline pilots regularly intercept eagles soaring high above the earth at heights few other birds could achieve. One raptor, the Lammergeier, can reach the staggering height of 25000 feet - five miles above the surface of the earth! Eagles have been spotted at sea between New York and England, soaring nonchalantly at great altitudes. One was spotted 900 miles south of Greenland, an area with virtually no land whatsoever. They soar so high, in fact, that ice sometimes forms upon their wings.

Eagles literally jump into the air, with some jumps attaining 15 feet or more, then with a powerful down beat of the wings the bird is airborne. An altitude of 12000 feet may be reached within minutes.

In conditions in which it would be difficult for a man to stand, an eagle can hover as steady as a rock, the wing tips moving constantly and automatically to make adjustments to the air currents. Indeed an eagle's mastery of flight is something to behold and it is probably this factor more than anything else that makes the bird such an outstanding creature. Eagles can dive at speeds of up to 200 kph, while in cross country flight they are capable to speeds of up to 100 kph. Bonelli's eagle will enter a 200 kph dive straight for its quarry, striking it in a spectacular mid air explosion of feathers. Quickly executing a neat dive, the bird rolls onto its back and catches the stunned prey in its deadly talons, all before the quarry hits the ground. A truly remarkable aerial feat and breathtaking to observe.

The Golden Eagle is a more graceful flyer than most and it is also one of the fiercest birds alive. Golden Eagle mates often hunt together, soaring high through the sky, using their remarkable vision - five times stronger than man's - to locate snakes and mice, flying in ever-widening circles and long sweeps until some movement is spotted. Then at an opportune moment the eagle will fold its powerful wings and slip into a screaming dive. Five yards from its prey it will suddenly spread its giant wings (they act like a brake), shoot out its cruel talons and seize its terrified victim. If the eagle fails to seize its prey it will proceed to drive it towards the hovering mate who then repeats the attack at the appropriate moment.

This powerful bird does much good, eliminating the land of rodents, snakes and rabbits. Even with desired species of wildlife the eagle helps to eliminate the weak and sickly, thus ensuring the quality of the breeding stock.

The eagle mounts the thermal current - he understands the thermals, the air currents more than any bird alive. As the eagle mounts the wind he is in control but the thermal provides the power, the lift to enable him to soar higher, longer and further.

Learn the facts of life and use them.

It is wonderful to observe the eagle. Early morning in the Australian desert finds them perched quietly on a craggy rock, escarpment or tree. The eagle instinctively knows the suns rays are not yet sufficient for it to warm the earth and create the necessary thermal currents for effortless flight.

Work smarter not harder.

The eagle waits. All other birds about him flap. Their ceaseless efforts and wing beating necessary to gain altitude in the cool desert morning does not manage to attract even the slightest interest from the "king of the sky". He remains perched quietly on his rocky citadel, completely aloof and disinterested in the comings and goings of the lesser creatures about him.

And still the eagle waits. By mid morning the desert sun has heated the ground temperature sufficiently to cause the thermal currents to begin to rise, their unseen hands spiral from the earth skyward. Suddenly, by some inner cue or sign, the magnificent wedge tail eagle spreads its awesome wings and virtually leaps into the air. Effortlessly but powerfully he flaps once, twice and then he is seized, engulfed by an unseen hand, the thermals.....and rises. Higher and higher, with just the merest flip of the wings, the giant bird soars. Higher, further and longer he soars than any other bird in the sky. He almost disappears from human view, a mere speck in the vast expanse of blue.

When the day ends and all other birds are tired, exhausted by their constant efforts to stay aloft, the eagle glides in for a perfect landing. Although he has soared through the sky for most of the day, he is relaxed poised and tireless. The thermals that bore him so high now return him gently back to earth.
The higher we soar the more we can observe and be

observed. An eagle at 10000 feet, as well as being observed, can see trouble or prey miles away, whereas a crow at 30 feet can spot things a mere few hundred yards away and a turkey, or chicken that never leaves the ground has virtually zero field of vision and is likely to perish in a brush fire or from some ravaging predator.

OPEN YOUR WINGS - IT'S SOARING TIME.

It's one thing to flap your wings and fly, it's another thing to soar.

You can enjoy a good life or a great life.

James Russell Lowell expressed it well -

> *Life is a leaf of paper white*
> *Whereon each one of us may write*
> *His word or two, and then comes night.*

> *Greatly begin! Though thou have time*
> *But for a line, be that sublime -*
> *Not failure, but low aim, is a crime.*

A parrot talks much, but flies little.

It's time to catch those thermal currents to lift you up where you belong - where eagles fly.

It's time to get the big picture of life. We must learn to look beyond the horizon.

I remember at one time, on a commercial plane, being invited to the cockpit. Night was falling and even though we were hundreds of miles from our destination, the pilot pointed out the lights of the city away in the distance. Because of our altitude we could see so far. Those travelling on the highway far below were only able to see the next bend in the road.

You must believe and see it in your mind's eye that you can soar. Your imagination is one of your greatest gifts and you need to cherish it.

Creative imagination is that part of the mind which generates desires, thoughts, hopes and dreams. Everything that has ever been achieved started first as an unseen spark in a creative imagination.

The part of your mind that plays the greatest role in achievement is that part of your mind that imagines. We spend years developing the part of the mind that reasons, memorises and learns, but almost no time is given to developing the immense potential of our imagination. Yet the untapped power of our imagination is unlimited.

The human brain is in two distinct parts, each having different functions. The left side of the brain is basically concerned with logic and speech - it thinks. The right side of the brain is related to intuition and creativity - it knows. It is visual in orientation. It is the right side of the brain that some of us tend to neglect.

People who learn to use their imagination flexibly see creatively. There is a rich source of ideas and mental pictures that can be developed.

A person's imagination reflects an ability to visualise something that has neither been seen nor experienced before. Use your imagination and mind to think like a winner.

THINK LIKE A WINNER

A winner is always ready to tackle something new. A loser is prone to believe it can't be done.

A winner isn't afraid of competition. A loser excuses himself with the idea that the competition beat him.

A winner knows he is sometimes wrong and is willing to admit his mistakes. A loser can usually find someone to blame.

A winner is challenged by a new problem. A loser doesn't want to face it.

A winner is decisive. A loser frustrates himself with indecision.

A winner realises there is no time like the present to get a job done. A loser is prone to procrastinate with the hope that things will be better tomorrow.

A winner thinks positively, acts positively and lives positively. A loser usually has a negative approach to everything.

So if you want to be a winner, **think** like a winner, **act** like a winner and, sooner than you think, you will **be** a winner.

Determine right now that you want to be a winner, that you want to be successful in life.

Here are some guidelines for success at any age:

* Seek, see and seize opportunities. Great chances and challenges don't always come gift-wrapped.

* Channel your passion into your profession.

* Persist and persevere. Overnight success is a myth.

* Be inquisitive. Read widely outside of your field. Ask questions and turn things inside out.

* Be optimistic. Things aren't always as hard to accomplish as you expect.

* Learn to get along with people. Make people like you.

* Learn to exhibit more patience than any other person you know.

* Respect other people's opinions and ideas.

* Learn to think problems through. Don't give up. If you don't get the answer today, go back to it tomorrow. Discipline your mind to the thought that anything given you to decide, pre-supposes your ability to solve it. Sufficient thought will bring the proper solution in due time.

* Learn to put yourself in the other person's place. There are two sides to every dispute and yours is not necessarily the right one. Keep an open mind, no matter how personal the point at issue.

* Be humble.

* Be loyal.

* Cultivate cheerfulness.

* Work hard.

* Find your own particular talent.

* Be big.

* Be honest.

* Live with enthusiasm.

* Don't let your possessions possess you.

* Don't worry about your problems.

* Look up to people when you can - down to no one.

* Don't cling to the past.

* Assume your full share of responsibility in the world.

* Strive to be happy and to enjoy life.

Success in life goes to the person who has the courage to dream, the ability to organise and the strength to execute.

The ladder of success does not care who climbs it.

Success in life has four main keys:

1. Commitment
2. Effort
3. Motivation
4. Discipline

Remember - even a mosquito doesn't get a slap on the back until she starts to work!

The greatest risk in life is to wait for, and depend upon, others for your security.

It's time for you to get the wind beneath your wings.

It's time for you to soar.

No one can predict to what heights you can soar. Even you will not know until you spread your wings.

Soaring Above The Winds Of Adversity

3. SOARING ABOVE THE WINDS OF ADVERSITY

As the eagle approaches a storm front it locks its wings into such a position as to allow the force of the buffeting wind to lift it, the forward motion of the wind striking the wings at just the right angle to cause the uplift. The force of the storm is deflected harmlessly downwards by those magnificent wings, allowing the bird to soar to new and greater heights. Rather than defeat the bird, rather than drain it of all its strength in a titanic battle to stay aloft, the eagle manoeuvres and glides about without so much as the barest effort, the merest flap of its huge wings. The eagle uses the force of the storm to its own advantage, harnessing the very power sent to destroy. The storm actually increases its speed.

There is going to be adversity coming along in your life and things are going to be at you all the time. You know, a kite only flies when the wind is against it and when you look back in your life it will be the tough times in life that you will really appreciate. They are the things that ultimately make you successful. Eagles have their tormentors, even the little birds come at them all the time. You can have people coming at you all the time, saying, "You can't do that." They may be close family or friends. "Who does he think he is?" "Who does she think she is?" "I know them, I went to school with them. Who are they to become successful in life?" Little tormentors - they are around you all the time. I had a little corgi dog once. He was very cheeky and used to run down the road to an alsatian. He would go up to the alsatian, look up in its eyes and start yapping away - yap, yap, yap! Now the alsatian looked down and didn't do a thing. It could have wiped that corgi off the face of the earth. But it didn't do it. Why? It knew that it was the bigger dog. It didn't have to prove a thing.

In cold climates eagles rarely migrate like most other birds, possessing the unique ability to persist and survive the rigours of winter, the cold winds of adversity. Not being weak, pathetic creatures, eagles have learned to withstand the "cold winds of adversity" and overcome great hardships in life.

Just as a diamond cannot be polished without friction, so a person cannot be perfected without trials.

Usually people do not fail, they just give up easily. It is

still true that when the going gets tough, the tough get going.

The person who expects to escape the pangs of suffering, adversity and disappointment simply has no knowledge of history or of life. The master musician knows that suffering precedes glory and acclaim. He knows the hours, days and months of gruelling practice and self-sacrifice that precede the one hour of perfect rendition when his mastership is applauded. The student knows that years of study, privation and self-renunciation precede the triumphant day of graduation and honours.

Dr Lambie, medical missionary, formerly of Abyssinia, has forded many swift and bridge-less streams in Africa. The danger in crossing such a stream lies in being swept off one's feet and carried down the stream to greater depths or hurled to death against the hidden rocks. Dr Lambie learned from the natives the best way to make such a hazardous crossing. The man about to cross finds a large stone, the heavier the better, lifts it to his shoulder and carries it across the stream as "ballast". The extra weight of the stone keeps his feet solid on the bed of the stream and he can cross safely without being swept away.

Dr Lambie drew this application:
While crossing the dangerous stream of life enemies constantly seek to overthrow us and rush us down to ruin. We need the ballast of burden-bearing, a load of affliction, to keep us from being swept off our feet.

When adversity and the tough times come (and they will!), just how do you handle them?

1. Stop blaming others or circumstances.
It's not the problem but how we react to the problem. Nobody is defeated until they start blaming someone else. Don't fix the blame - fix the problem.

2. Clearly analyse the problem.
(a)   Identify the problem.
(b)   Predict what the problem will do if you don't do anything about it.
(c)   Decide on your response from all the options and alternatives.
Then:
(d)   Execute and act on the most positive option you can imagine.

Is your problem a financial one? Put on your thinking cap again. Usually it is not a money problem but an idea problem.

3. Take action.
Turn the lemon into lemonade! Every obstacle can be an opportunity.
Get moving - don't sit in a heap. Do something. Get advice. Every problem is loaded with possibilities. Get enthusiastic.

<u>4.</u> <u>Take control</u>.
Don't allow circumstances to control you.
Don't allow people to control you.
Don't allow your background, race or lack of education to control you.
Don't have fences or ceilings in your life.
Don't throw in the towel to fear or frustration or fatigue.
Don't surrender to the gloom-doom merchants of life.
Take control of your own destiny because today's decisions are tomorrow's realities.

Take a lesson from the eagle. Use adversity to further develop you to become even more successful with your life.

Birds Of Light

4. BIRDS OF LIGHT

Eagles are birds of the light. They hunt by day, they fly by day and they feed by day. They are truly creatures of the light.

Eagles are remarkably clean birds, preferring to kill their own prey which usually consists of fish, rabbits, squirrels and other small game. In fact these birds in their natural setting have little appetite for decaying and rotting flesh that attracts crows, vultures and other scavengers. Vultures and buzzards have featherless necks and heads to enable them to feed inside dead carcasses.

However, eagles can become dirty birds. In fact, most eagles destined to a life of captivity resort to such with little thought for their appearance, habits and food. When caged this beautiful bird can sink to a place where it will eat almost anything - carrion, rotting meat, the rubbish and stinking offal. The bird ceases to wash and preen itself, becomes moody and bad tempered, a far cry from its original lifestyle.

It seems that eagles have high standards. They want the best in life, not the rubbish.

If you want to fly with the eagles you must strive for the very best. There must be a commitment to excellence.

Those who desire to soar with eagles should love excellence and shun mediocrity. Excellence is not achieved by accident. What we aim at determines what we will become and, while we may not always make our goals, our goals will always make us.

To aim at excellence is to point your life toward the realisation of your potential, the fulfilment of your capabilities.

Excellence is an unending pursuit   Tom Landry of the "Dallas Cowboys" was so right when he observed, "The quality of a life is in direct proportion to its commitment to excellence."

Running to win involves a consuming desire to be the best we can be.

Michelangelo stands as one of the towering figures in the history of art. His majestic frescoes on the ceiling of the Sistine Chapel and his masterful sculptures bear witness to his greatness. But he was a man never content to rest on his laurels. He spent countless hours on his back on the scaffolding in the Sistine, carefully perfecting the details of each figure. When a friend questioned such meticulous attention to detail on the grounds that "at that height who will know whether it is perfect or not?", Michelangelo's simple response was, "I will." After completing what some consider his greatest work, *Moses*, the master sculptor stood back and surveyed his craftsmanship. Suddenly, in anger, he struck the knee of his creation with his chisel and shouted, "Why don't you speak?" The chisel scar that remains on the statue's knee is the mark of a man who always reached out for more. His ambition was to be the best he could be.

The difference between good and great is a little extra effort.

Excellence demands quality in leadership, products, performance, or lifestyle. True success demands quality. The day of junk presentation is over. Study any winner. It is not their cleverness, but the fact that each and every aspect of their business, life or performance, is just a touch better than the norm. Don't try to be one thousand percent better at one thing. Be one percent better at one thousand things.

As valuable as they may be, computers can tell you so much but it is only the human being that can really tell quality in a product or performance.

Don't make the mistake of running a business or organisation on figures and finances alone or you will go under. Quality is the key.

George Allan, former coach of the Washington Redskins Football Team, is often quoted as saying, "I demand of my men that they give 110 percent." On that football field he insists his men give far more than they think they are capable of giving.

The best way to better our lot is to do a lot better.

Vince Lombardi was committed to excellence. He stated, "I would like to say that the quality of any man's life has got to be full measure of that man's personal commitment to excellence and to victory, regardless of what fields he may be in."

The difference between ordinary and extraordinary is that little extra. This is excellence.

The day of the junk, second rate, "that's near enough" presentation is over. The achiever must strive for excellence.

You're flying free, you're an eagle. Set those high standards of integrity and excellence. Become a quality person.

Be the best you personally can be. Why not? What do you have to lose? There is everything to gain. Class up your act and get that mind under control. Carry yourself like the achiever you really are.

You are an eagle. Fly like one.

Vision

5. VISION

Two sets of eyelids

Eagles have two sets of eyelids to protect their extremely keen sight. One set is used while the bird is stationary or on the earth, but the instant the eagle is airborne a second set of eyelids or translucent nictitating membranes drop over the powerful eyes. This is not only to protect the bird from the onrushing air (when in speeding dives) but also against trees, bushes and even the prey itself. The sun too can cause problems, especially at the altitudes the big raptors attain. The membrane is drawn across their eyes to keep them clean.

Eagles have remarkably developed eyesight which includes both sideways and binocular vision. An eagle soaring hundreds of feet above the ground can detect the movement of a tiny field mouse. Its eyes adjust quickly and accurately with depth of field and focus. So great is the eagle's power of sight that it can survey a five-mile area with great accuracy. Its scope of vision is 275 degrees, enabling the bird to observe either side and gain a perspective of anything approaching from the rear as well. The eyes are not fully developed at birth but develop with maturity.

The eagle can readily identify its prey at about 1 mile, but by moving its head it increases the range to almost double.

The eagle's ability to obtain great heights gains him a two-fold advantage. One to observe storms and dangers afar off, two to observe prey and food. Birds such as crows and turkeys rarely achieve great heights and have limited vision. It's the same for us in life.

Eagles possess the ability to distinguish colours - a fact unusual in the animal kingdom. Actually they see colour with a far greater clarity than humans, which makes them much more aware of the beauty of the earth. Another remarkable feature of their sight is the pectens inside their eyes which act as a gyroscope enabling them to navigate with extreme accuracy. An eagle's eyes are set far apart on each side of its head, allowing depth perception, highly advantageous when judging heights and distances. In screaming dives of 100mph the bird must judge distances quickly and accurately before disaster strikes.

It is simply a fact of life - the higher you fly, the further you see.

However, you can fly high but not be equipped to see further down the road. Even the eyes of the eagle are not fully developed at birth. I hope by now you are starting to catch the excitement and are realising the great potential of your life. More than just seeing, I trust you are developing great VISION.

A dynamic life is always fired by vision.

If you can imagine it, you can achieve it.

If you can dream it, you can become it.

A tourist in Switzerland was taken by a local guide on a mountain climb. At one point the guide disturbed his client by urging: "Be careful not to fall here because it is very dangerous. But if you do fall, remember to look to the right - the view is the best for miles around!" Actually it is when we get the full view that we really start to soar in life.

There was a man out west who caught an eagle and kept it in confinement for 17 years. At last, having to move a distance, he advertised to sell all his goods at auction and that at the close of the sale he would liberate this old eagle, captive for so long. People came for hundreds of miles to see the bird set free. The auction was over. Low clouds hung over the earth, dark and drear. The cage was opened but the eagle did not move. His master called him. Still he stayed inside.

At last his master pulled him out and, with all his strength, tried to push the bird toward the zenith. His great wings only spread to allow him to settle back to the man's shoulder. The man was nonplussed. Just then there shot through the clouds a bright beam of sunshine, straight to the eagle's eye. And the eagle rose as if by magnet towards the source.

Once you catch that beam of sunshine in your eye, once you catch the vision of the full potential of your life, then you will really begin to fly.

The poorest person is not the one without a cent, but rather the one without a dream.

You only have one life, one shot at it - make big plans.

Life is filled with challenges and opportunities, mountains to be climbed and conquered with others to follow. When you are no longer interested in climbing mountains, to see other mountains to climb, life is over.

Vision sees the invisible, believes the incredible and receives the impossible.

Without vision you are just playing games with your life.

Men and women with vision see more and further than others. They have empires in their brains.

"You're as big as you think!" So reads the caption to an advertisement in one of the larger magazines. The picture is of a boy gazing into the future. In the background there is a whirling planet and a rocket bursting out into space. The caption is explained in a short paragraph:

"Only a boy. But his thoughts are far in the future. Thinking, dreaming, his mind sees more than his eyes do. So with all boys... Vision, looking beyond the common place, finds new things to do. And growth, as it always must, follows where mind marks the way."

"Man's mind, stretched to a new idea, never goes back to its original dimensions." [Olivia Wendell Holmes]

You can't think in terms of catching mice and expect to catch lions.

> Small minds discuss persons.
> Average minds discuss events.
> Great minds discuss ideas.

"As a man thinks in his heart, so is he."

Your imagination is one of the most powerful things you possess. Imagination is your dream machine. Leaders organise special dream times. Time to dream big dreams.

The tragedy today is that we crush the ability of our children to dream by demanding that they grow up too soon. Real leaders have never lost that childlike ability to dream dreams.

Helen Keller, that wonderful blind and deaf person, said, "The greatest tragedy to befall a person is to have sight but lack vision."

IT IS SO TRUE THAT POOR EYES LIMIT A MAN'S SIGHT; POOR VISION, HIS DEEDS.

There is nothing that excites and motivates people like a vision to accomplish something special. Study great people and you will find they have been dreamers.

"When you cease to dream, you cease to live."
[Malcolm S Forbes]

Start dreaming and keep on dreaming. If your dream ever gets foggy set some time aside to resharpen your vision. Have a dream worth dreaming. Most of us have vast potential that has never been developed, simply because we failed to recognise it, or the circumstances in our life have never required it.

Dreams are like a huge motivational magnet. They help you through life's low points.

Constantly dare to dream, not only personally, but also on

the team level. If you want your life and those you work with, to be vital in the future, spend time letting your imagination soar.

If you had anything you wanted - unlimited time, unlimited money, unlimited information, unlimited wisdom, unlimited staff - all the resources you could ask for - what would you do? Your answer to that question is your dream.

Vision is a comprehensive sense of where you are, where you are going, how you are going to get there and what you will do after you get there. It is dreaming dreams about the future. It is seeing the big picture and personally painting a part of it.

Vision is feeling challenged by the world around and being compelled to make a mark on it through the force of your own ideas, personality, resources and desires.

Vision must be focused. If it is too broad people will flounder and become discouraged. If it is non-specific it is useless. It must be clear, concise and in focus. Blurry vision causes people to lose their way.

Without limiting the vision, at the same time it must be attainable. Set realistic reachable goals, otherwise you will become discouraged and will discourage others.

We need visionaries who will embark on high-risk ventures. History is full of them and we are the better for it today.

It's people who have vision. Programmes don't have vision. All too often we take the spirit out of visionaries.

Vision starts very much out of attitude and attitude determines altitude. What dreams and visions keep you awake at night? What fresh idea would revolutionise your life? How can you develop this idea so that others will get excited about joining you in changing your world?

Forget the cynics and the knockers. They will always be around in abundance to knock you. There will always be the discouragers and the doubters who can't see beyond the first obstacle. People of vision are not afraid to fail.

"The tragedy of life is not that we die, but what dies inside a man while he lives."   [Albert Schweitzer]

A person with vision is one who has the courage to dream, the ability to organise and the strength to execute the action necessary. A leader is simply one who knows where they want to go, gets up and goes.

"Neither you nor the world knows what you can do until you have tried."   [Ralph Waldo Emerson]

NOTICE THREE VITAL THINGS ABOUT VISION

1. Vision creates power. The enthusiasm that comes from vision results in dynamic power. This then leads to greater productivity and feelings of productivity

increase your feelings of self-esteem. Enthusiasm is produced from vision and the power from enthusiasm is the energy that drives every successful idea.

2. Great vision comes from being quiet, still, often alone, to spend time in solitude and reflection. We live in a crazy rat-race world. Find a place where you can enjoy solitude. In a quiet place will come your best ideas.

3. Never allow your vision to escape you. Just as a fire will die without fuel, so too will your visions and dreams unless you keep them constantly alive. Your vision should be so much part of you that you are living it day by day. Each day you need to rehearse and go over your vision. Visions rebuild themselves in quietness, not in the hustle and bustle of life.

"We grow by dreams. All big men are dreamers. Some of us let dreams die, but others nourish and protect them, nurse them through bad days...to the sunshine and light which always comes.   [Woodrow Wilson]

It's time for you to push your wings a little harder, to fly above the trees, the hills, the mountains. The higher you fly, the better the view.

A dynamic life is always fired by vision.

Develop vision like an eagle.

Focus

6. FOCUS

Once the prey is located the bird develops singleness of mind and purpose. From that moment on every part of its powerful, beautiful body is locked into line with the focus of those keen eyes. The wings, the talons, the beak, the understanding of aerodynamics, all come into line with that one thought - to catch the prey. Once locked onto that quarry, the eagle will use everything it possesses, in other words, it goes into the fray wholeheartedly, giving all in the pursuit. Nothing will cause it to deviate from its course, even annoyance from smaller foes will not interrupt its powerful attack.

Singleness of Purpose

Having gained a vision for the tremendous potential of your life, now that you are soaring with the eagles, it is vital that you do not allow distractions to enter your life.

Keep your dream ever before you. Pin up those photos. Write down your dreams and visions and review them constantly.

Don't zig-zag through life. You are now switching from sail-power to engine-power in reaching your destination. You are no longer at the mercy of the wind. Focus will take you to where you want to go.

I would sooner be a pile driver than a confetti sprinkler!

Watch those distractions

What are some of the distractions that could rob you of your dreams?

1. Obstacles

    Obstacles are the things you see when you take your eyes off the goals. If you come to a mountain, climb on it, go round it, tunnel through it! Don't allow it to stop you. The railway lines between East and West America and in Australia would never have been accomplished if those building them had stopped because of the mountains, rivers and vast plains. They crossed them all. Cross those obstacles in your life. Opportunities never come to those who wait. They are captured by those who dare to attack.

    Don't allow the obstacles to defeat you. Obstacles instead will make you, steel you, develop you.

2. Criticism

If you are in the front line you will be the first to get shot at! Of course you will be criticised. Turkeys would sooner gobble, gobble, gobble all day than fly, but see what they miss. Go check your local city park. There has never been a statue erected to a critic!

There are those, sadly, who take pot shots, for no reason, at the soaring eagles. You will be vulnerable as you begin to soar, but would an eagle trade places with a turkey?!

If criticism is levelled at you, analyse it. If there is something you can learn that will help you - good, use it. Otherwise throw it behind you and keep going. You cannot afford the luxury of carrying excess baggage.

3. Circumstances

We are good at pinning the blame for our lack of accomplishment on others or on circumstances. History is filled with inspiring stories of those who fought against the odds and won. Don't allow health, ethnic background, where you were born, lack of opportunities as a child, lack of education - the list could go on and on - to hinder you. I heard a blind man say recently that blindness was not a restriction, just a bit of a nuisance at times.

4.   Others

Other people can take your focus off your dreams as well. Our loved ones can hold us back. Even our friends often cannot appreciate our desire to achieve in life. So many are drawn off target just fearing what others (whoever they are!) are thinking. Don't become a slave to the opinions of others. Is an eagle going to ask a turkey how high he is allowed to fly?!

Focus on your dreams by controlling your time

When an eagle is on the attack it does not have time at that moment to check the views in another valley. This is focus time.

Achievers have a strong sense of urgency.

Time is your most valuable personal resource. Use it wisely because it cannot be replaced.

Time management skills can be developed and perfected and will lead you on to greater productivity and performance.

Here are a few well known tips for daily time planning:

*   Create a daily "to do" list. (It is best to write it out the night before.)

* List goals and set priorities - A - B - C.

* Do A's first.

* Handle each piece of paper once only.

* Do it now!

* Right now, what is the best use of my time?

Disciplined focus is what distinguishes those who make things happen from those who watch things happen.

Here are some of the techniques used by successful achievers to make the best use of their most precious commodity - time.

A. Do the most important things first. Sometimes we avoid difficult or disagreeable tasks. Force yourself to do these tasks first then reward yourself. Don't waste time on unimportant things. Very little can stand against sustained, single minded, pursuit of your goals.

B. Don't try to do everything at once. Focus only on the areas that will benefit most from your expertise. Concentrate on a few things at a time. Stick to them until you are satisfied they are under control.

C. Limit interruptions as much as possible. Guard your best working times. If necessary work on a problem in a secluded area. Interruptions are the number one time wasters.

D. Handle your mail promptly. Unattended mail causes stress. Set time aside when you will open and attend to your mail. Procrastination results in mail accumulating, requiring action. Throw away unnecessary mail, give it to your secretary, or send it to the required department for their action.

E. Set deadlines. This will force you to accomplish projects quickly.

F. Think - how can I do it better? Set quality time aside to think about creative ways to improve the performance of your organisation. Peak performance comes through pondering. This may well prove to be invaluable to you. When you are relaxed brainstorm your situation. You will be amazed at the ideas that spring to light. The achiever, as well as having vision, must inspire others.

G. You don't have to attend every meeting. Be very selective regarding meetings. Probably about half of them you don't need to attend. Maybe someone else can go in your place and give you a report. Whatever meetings you do attend, encourage brevity.

H. Control visitors. There is often a fine line in sharing time and wasting time. "Can I have a moment of your time?" is the opening line that can interrupt valuable time. You want to keep the lines of communication open but not waste time.

It may be possible to have a "holding station", a lounge or area that is not in your office. Once people are in your office it is hard to get them to leave. You may find it helpful to remain standing if it is just small talk. People get down to business faster when they are on their feet. Perhaps you can organise a more suitable time to meet them later. It is very important that you don't appear impolite.

I. Invest your time where it pays the most. Often we invest huge amounts of time where there is little return for the effort. You may have to spend time doing some honest thinking to analyse your time investments. Do not waste your high energy hours. Invest them where they produce the highest payoff.

J. Delegate responsibility. Achievers make the most use of their time by sharing the workload. Then you must allow your team to put their personal stamp on projects assigned to them. Try and set completion times for accomplishment.

K. Don't allow worry to distract you. Worry is like a rocking chair, it will give you something to do but it won't get you anywhere!

You can slice your worries in half by asking the following questions :-

What is the real problem?
What is the cause of the problem?
What are all the possible solutions to the problem?
What solution is the best?

L. Keep your mind on the project in hand. Too often, as we work on a particular project, our minds drift off on to some other thing we know that needs doing. It is important to discipline our minds to keep on with what we are doing at that moment.

M. Keep paper and pen handy to record inspirational thoughts. You may wake during the night with a great idea. Write it down straight away. A thought may come to you as you work on another project. Write it down straight away. This will help you to keep your mind on the subject and also that precious thought will not escape. The old saying is true that a blunt pencil will always remember more than a sharp mind.

N. Use travel time. Waiting for a plane, driving, picking up your children, can all be used to redeem time by reading, listening to a tape or having someone with you to invest time into their life. The most successful achievers never waste a moment.

O. Spend time relaxing. Holidays or days off are not wasted time. They are called recreation. And you do need to be re-created to be an effective achiever.

P. Use the telephone correctly. Write down a quick agenda before you use the phone (especially if it is long distance). Remember, the telephone is your servant. Sometimes you may have to ignore it completely or take it off the hook. Maybe your secretary or spouse can screen the calls for you. Train your team to use a fax machine. That way you have an accurate record.

The advantages of management

When you control your time you accomplish important goals and free up your nights and weekends for other family activities. Controlling your time helps overcome frustration and brings your life into balance and order, giving you the feeling of control and poise. Better planning of your time enables you to give yourself more to others. You feel better on top of the pile than under it. Life will take on a greater zest, enthusiasm and productivity. You will be able to handle a crisis far more easily and it will give you more time for planning.

Focus like the eagle and don't allow your dreams to escape you.

Chapter

7

Goalsetting

7. GOALSETTING

An eagle's nest is a sight to behold. Usually perched high in the mountains, on the face of some sheer cliff or rock wall or the highest tree about, the nest is located in the most remote, unattainable spot that the bird can find. The nest can be so huge that it will support two grown men. In fact the nest itself can weigh in excess of 2 tonnes. Now remembering that each and every solitary stick has to be carried to this remote building site by the eagle, one can get some idea of the monumental size of the task. (The eagle remodels the nest each year until it may hold thousands of sticks as well as timber from construction sites and discarded cloth, clothing and paper. Should the nest become dirty, fresh sticks, grass and leaves are carried up and piled on top of the old floor.)

But the eagle is not overwhelmed or overawed by the sheer immensity of the job; in-built within the bird is the blueprint for the future nest. God has given the eagle a picture of exactly what the nest will look like and the way to go about making the image a reality. Nothing deters the eagle from bringing that blueprint into reality, neither seemingly insurmountable odds, adversities or simple temporary setbacks. In the face of storms, fires, blizzards, earthquakes - no matter how often the nest is destroyed, the eagle continues. He presses on towards the mark, never looking back to past failures. You will never see a partly completed eagle's nest. The bird always finishes the job.

There are plenty that have been broken down and destroyed or partly destroyed, but never one that the eagle has abandoned because the going was too tough. The eagle is certainly no weakling. He always succeeds because he has that inner picture, that goal, that vision imprinted deeply within him and so he presses on again and again with perseverance and patience until that picture becomes a reality. We need that vision, that picture embedded strongly within us and then the perseverance to press on until we see it come to pass.

Yet an eagle will struggle and persevere against all odds. If the nest is blown down - as nests constantly are - the eagle will rebuild and rebuild and rebuild again if necessary. The reason the eagle succeeds is because he thinks he can. He can do it because he thinks he can.

He is an eagle, so he acts like an eagle. Come rain, come hail, come storm, come man, come fire, come anything -

the eagle will rebuild the nest until he succeeds.

Goalsetting and the achiever

Goals are vision with feet. Goals are a set of specific, measurable steps to achieve the vision. When realistic goals are set and met, you will feel satisfied and successful. The whole concept of setting goals will have the exciting flavour of accomplishment. Goalsetting will deliver you from crisis management. You switch from fire fighting to fire prevention.

Goalsetting will help you to constantly resharpen your vision. An axeman never loses time sharpening his axe. Take time to hone and rehone your goals.

Here are some of the benefits of goalsetting:

1. <u>Goals simplify the decision-making process.</u>
   The achiever is constantly faced with a multitude of decisions. Invitations to join this Board or that, to speak at conventions and meetings, a thousand and one opportunities come. His/her gift makes way for them. Others feel they can organise your life better than you can. When you know your direction in life as you establish goals, so you can evaluate simply and easily each situation as it presents itself.

2. <u>Goals tone up mental and physical health.</u>
   The reason so many people die soon after retirement

is that they have ceased to set goals for themselves. Without direction in your life you are vulnerable to negative thought patterns. It is well known that your mental attitude and your physical health are closely related. Having set goals will demand that you keep sharp, mentally and physically in shape.

3. Goals generate respect.

4. Goals help you to realise and enjoy the feeling of accomplishment. What you cannot measure you cannot monitor. Without goals you float aimlessly, but as you achieve your goals there is a feeling of satisfaction and accomplishment.

5. Goals produce persistence.
   Persistence, or staying power, is the quality that sets the leader apart. Just as the stamp sticks to the letter until it gets there, so the achiever never gives up.

   Eagles are remarkably patient birds, a quality that seems almost obsolete in this day of instant coffee, instant food, instant delivery - instant everything. Yet this bird, with its mastery of flight, its deadly beak and razor sharp talons, its extra keen eyesight and legendary boldness has great need for this quality of patience. During hunting, often the eagle will miss its prey and would otherwise go hungry but for its ability to quietly and patiently wait it out. Eagles have been observed roosting for hours above a rabbit hole, snake hole or place where a fish or bird had disappeared. The raptor will wait and wait, sometimes for hours on end. Usually the bird's patience is rewarded and the prey will show its head and, like lightning, the eagle strikes with devastating speed and power.

Problems and discouragements will face the achiever, but he can overcome them with staying power.

Many times we are nearer our goals than we think we are, so never give up - persist. It's always too soon to quit.

6. <u>Goals deliver the achiever from the deception and desire to applause.</u>
   Achievers become unstuck when they start to believe their own publicity! It is always a fact of life that a third of the crowd care for you, a third of the crowd don't care for you and the other third couldn't care less about you! That should bring you down to earth.

7. <u>Goals deliver you from living in the past.</u>
   An achiever, often because of his hard work, will receive justified praise. The problem arises when his ego needs to feed on it.

Having set goals the leader takes his mind off the past and centres his attention on the future.

The advantages of goalsetting

The establishment of a goals' programme is the way you can fulfil your vision. Setting goals is not a one-time exercise. It is an ongoing discipline. Without a goals' programme a vision is only wishful thinking. Your goals will have to be constantly modified. While you are working on your immediate, or short-range goals, you must be careful to keep your eyes on your long-range goals.

Your vision must remain permanent but your goals must remain flexible. Do not change the order. Far too many allow their vision to change and make their goals permanent.

It is time now to practically and systematically set out your goals. Remember, goals are a set of specific, measurable steps that design the programme for fulfilling your vision.

1. Make a list of your goals.
   Write down all the goals that you can think of in the four areas - being - doing - owning - accomplishing. Start with 20 years then 15, then 10, then 5, then 1 year, then 6 months, then 90 days, then 60 days.

2. Now rearrange them in order of priority for each of the four areas. Select the goals you want first. Next set a target date. Be realistic. Make them attainable goals. A goal without a deadline is not really a goal...it

is a wish.

3. Make a list of the required action you must take to achieve your goal. For example the extra effort required, or more study, or the cash needed. (Remember - no gain without pain)

4. Develop the qualities in your personal behaviour that will be required. Obtain the skills. For example - a pleasant personality, neat appearance, mental awareness, a winning smile, a warm handshake, a positive walk or plain hard work.

5. List your deficiencies and conquer them, starting right now! Today!

6. List the personnel or help needed to achieve your goals and the techniques or methods as well.

7. Develop an iron will determination to follow through your plans regardless of obstacles, criticism or circumstances, or what other people say, think or do.

8. Visualise the new you. Vividly imagine yourself as having already reached your goals.

9. Begin at once.

In the absence of clearly defined goals we are forced to concentrate on activity and ultimately become enslaved by it. Remember, there is no joy in victory without running the risk of defeat.

<u>Opportunities never come to those who wait - they are captured by those who dare to attack.</u>

The fulfilment of our goals must be good for others. If they bring harm to others, then our goals are selfish. The great rewards in life are love and achievement. All else is secondary. Become a giver - not a getter.

Don't be afraid to set goals.

To achieve goals demands hard work, determination and commitment. For many, though, the main reason they do not establish a quest to achieve goals is plain fear; the fear of ridicule from others or the fear of defeat. Others fear their goals will not be perfect - or worse still, they may consider themselves presumptuous.

The importance and the benefit of goalsetting is immeasurable. Without setting goals your visions and dreams are just wishful thinking. There are so many benefits in goalsetting. They make decision making easier. Your physical and mental health are better. You have established a positive attitude to life. You are helping to eliminate stress, confusion and fear. Those who have goals attract respect from people. It gives you a sense of accomplishment. It gives you "stickability" and staying power. It is staying power that sets the leader apart.

The tragedy of life doesn't lie in not reaching your goal; the tragedy lies in having no goal to reach.

Henry Kaiser said, "Determine what you want more than anything else in life, write down the means by which you intend to attain it and permit nothing to deter you from pursuing it."

Without goals and priorities we will never escape the tyranny of the urgent. If we do not have our eyes fixed on a goal the urgent will crowd out the important.

The only difference between being a "dreamer" and a "goalsetter" is adding a deadline to the dream.

Goalsetting accomplishes your vision.

You're an eagle - act like an eagle. Start now. Set your goals and accomplish them.

Chapter

8

Enjoying Life

8. ENJOYING LIFE

Sense of Humour

Eagles indulge themselves in the very joy and thrill of living. They often soar and wheel about the sky, diving and zooming through the clouds for the sheer joy and pleasure. Take the time one day to observe how they use the thermal currents to soar high into the blue, then folding their wings tightly by their sides, they plunge toward the ground at breakneck speed pulling out of the dive just feet from the ground and then skimming over the surface of the earth. Eagles swoop in mock attack on birds and animals, sending them scurrying for cover. Yet all the time they have no intention of attacking the frightened quarry. You can almost hear them chuckle as they soar back into their heavenly habitat. Often they wheel and dart about for the pure pleasure of flying.

Learn to laugh

One of the first signs of mental breakdown is the inability to laugh.

Our world today is on an endless search for real joy and happiness. Ask anyone what they want most in life and most will reply - "I want to be happy."

If only happiness were as contagious as the common cold! Don't keep looking for happiness, give it and it will come to you. Happiness is not a station you arrive at, but the way you travel. King George V of England would say, "The secret of happiness is not in doing what one likes, but in liking what one has to do."

"It isn't your position that makes you happy or unhappy; it's your disposition."

Scientists have been studying the effects of laughter on human beings and have found, among other things, that laughter has a profound and instantaneous effect on virtually every important organ on the human body. Laughter reduces health-sapping tensions and relaxes the tissues as well as exercising the most vital organs. It is said that laughter, even when forced, results in beneficial effects on us, both mentally and physically. So next time you feel nervous and jittery indulge in a good laugh.

"It takes 72 muscles to frown - and only 14 to smile."

A 12-year-old girl in Winnipeg, Canada held a smile on her face for 10 hours, 5 minutes, establishing a new world record. She broke the longest smile record in the Guinness Book of World Records which was 7 hours, 32 minutes.

Not long ago there appeared in the newspapers the story of a little boy who had come in contact with a live electric wire. It touched one side of his face, burning and paralysing it. In court the boy's lawyer asked the little fellow to turn toward the jury and smile. He tried. One side of his face smiled but the injured side revealed a hideous and pitiful contortion. The jury took just twenty minutes to award the boy twenty thousand dollars. That was certified as the legal value of a smile.

Charles H Spurgeon, the great preacher, was emphasising to his class the importance of making the facial expression harmonise with the speech. "When you speak of Heaven," he said, "let your face light up, let it be irradiated with a heavenly gleam, let your eyes shine with reflected glory. But when you speak of hell - well, then, your ordinary face with do!"

Mother Teresa of Calcutta said, "True holiness consists of doing the will of God with a smile." Someone observed her ministering on those putrid streets and made the comment that she had never met anybody so joyful. She was asked, "How do you do this awful work?" She responded, "Awful work? What do you mean? I'm

immensely privileged. I'm serving my Lord - tangibly."
Her joy is legendary.

Let me list a few practical points to help you maintain real
joy and happiness.

1. <u>Count your blessings</u>

Learn to count your blessings and not your burdens. Come
with me to Bangladesh where it floods through your house
several times each year. Or to Nairobi in Kenya to walk
through one of the biggest slums in the world. Or to
Russia, where 73 years of communism have caused them
to eke out a living on a day-by-day basis. Right now there
are millions who would give anything to trade places with
you. Become successful so you can help them.

*"We must have sympathy for the loser. We must help the
poor. But let us also cheer for the doer, the achiever."*
[Vince Lombardi]

Should this continually put us on a guilt trip? No. Why
should we continually apologise for the blessing that has
been brought about by free enterprise?

The Good Samaritan could only help the one beaten and
robbed because he had money in his purse.

One of the biggest problems of the western world is an
ungrateful spirit.

Let us count our blessings - not our burdens.

Develop a gratitude attitude.

2. <u>Learn to live in the NOW</u>

Sometimes we can be so obsessed with the future that we forget to enjoy the <u>NOW</u>. Enjoy your family NOW. Have fun NOW. Let your family, partner, friends see you enjoying life.

3. <u>The great key to real joy is serving others</u>

Some people are bad spellers, they spell "service" - "serve-us"!

Life is a double-win. The more we help others, the further we all go.

4. <u>Joy and happiness are a CHOICE</u>

We can choose to be miserable, we can choose to allow worry and fear to dominate our lives, or we can make a deliberate choice for joy and happiness.

Yes - I know life is tough. Yes - I know it is difficult. Yes - I know things are unfair. There is only one good thing about misery - it's optional!

Life is a challenge. Tackle it with joy. That joy will be the secret of your strength.

Are you going to soar like an eagle or scratch like a turkey?

The choice is yours.

Chapter

9

Love Song

9.LOVE SONG

Eagle Courtship

Here once again we can learn from the eagle, the king of birds. Eagles mate for life - a fact not common in the animal kingdom. No matter what happens (short of death) the marriage will last, but not only last, the birds actually put their maximum effort into making it work. Eagles carry out a very elaborate courtship, one that does not cease at mating but will continue on throughout their life together. Man could learn much from this wonderful bird especially in the area of marriage relationships. It is almost as if the male eagle never takes his mate for granted but continues to court her for the rest of her life. In fact, besides the amorous attention the male shows her, he will also help with much of the "housework" such as hunting for their food, feeding and caring for the young.

The eagle's courtship takes place, naturally, in the sky where the bird is most at ease. The very best powers of flight are reserved for displays of affection. Occasionally the birds will even loop the loop - no mean feat for a bird. The two soar and dive in a breathtaking display of power and agility. Gradually they begin to interlock in flight, performing rolling somersaults in mid air and engaging in incredible aerial aerobatic feats together. Their "love songs" echo across their domain. Even normally silent species of eagles resort to love calls.

During the spectacular mid air display the female may carry a stick high into the air and drop it. The male responding to the gesture, will dive and retrieve it. This process may be repeated over and over again. The highlight of the performance is when the male dives at the female and she rolls on her back in mid air, flashing her deadly talons - not in a sign of hostility, but one of love - reaching out to one another. The two then clasp talons and engage in a series of cartwheels locked together, as they roll and plummet toward the earth.

It is a beautiful sight and sound to observe the eagles' courtship flight high above the earth as they swoop and glide in unison. Hovering and somersaulting together in their nuptial display, their love calls drifting out across the valleys and plains. Their flight together is a picture of grace, like ballet dancers who glide together across the face of the sky. In their downward rush they are undoubtedly one of the swiftest and most magnificent sights to behold in the bird kingdom. The mating vows are full of joy and are exchanged high above the earth in a realm few creatures ever attain. It is a vow of complete and total trust in each other - even to the death.

Devoted Partners

Although this courtship flight takes place at the time of mating, many species of eagle regularly (throughout their lifetime) perform this love ritual as a sign of devotion, affection and to strengthen the bond between the two. The bond is very strong and is cemented firmer with the passing years. A mated couple rarely fight and will join together in the face of adversity, threat, danger and even for the simple pleasure of hunting and soaring together. They are the classic mates, besides being lovers and parents they are friends - happy in each other's company. Often while the female sits on the nest, the male bird will quietly and gently groom and stroke her feathers. Of course it is impossible to say what the bird's motives are, but I would like to believe that it is simply a sign of affection. The male may even take a turn at "baby sitting" the eggs and should something disastrous happen to the mate, the male will even raise the young alone. That's dedication, that's commitment!

Almost every day the male eagle leaves the nest in search of a twig of greenery. Realising that some birds nest in barren desert areas, this may entail long sweeps of the countryside to locate a suitable bush or tree. Once located, the male eagle selects a prime sprig of greenery (new life) and flies back to the nest to present his mate with his "gift of love".

Family Protection

Eagles are not only devoted to each other but also to their families, going to great lengths to feed, protect, provide for and educate their young - a perfect role model of parents.

Adult eagles usually control an area of up to three miles, which they consider their private domain and while certain comings and goings will be allowed, no threat to the eyrie will be tolerated. Male eagles advertise their territories by soaring aloft and performing a series of spectacular undulations, diving, rolling, climbing and looping the loop, all accompanied by loud calls. A sort of eagle "show off" or display of powers. Eagles are bold birds at any time, but while protecting their young they are utterly fearless and will launch themselves into attack at the slightest provocation, to which many would-be birdwatchers and egg collectors can bear witness. Accounts of dogs being badly torn and mutilated are not uncommon.

How to date your mate

Here are some crazy ideas that just might work to add some spice and make that marriage soar! (Please don't check with my wife to see if we have tried them all!)

✪ Take some time aside and go through your old photos.

✪ Cook dinner together, recipes that you have never tried before.

✪ Read a good book together and discuss it.

✪ Go for a drive on a road you have never used before.

✪ Go for a walk and talk together.

✪ Go riding bikes together.

✪ Try a new sport together.

✪ Go sailing or boating.

✪ Go fishing.

✪ Do a fitness workout together.

✪ Go on a honeymoon memory date - talk over all the details.

✪ Give each other a back, head and foot rub.

✪ Kidnap your partner - plan it well in advance with family.

✪ Enjoy a romantic candle-lit dinner together with soft music.

✪ Work on a project on the house together.

✪ Go to the library and study a subject together.

✪ Take a study course together.

✪ Go on a marriage enrichment seminar.

✪ Go out with another couple.

✪ Play your favourite game together (buy some new ones)

✪ Go to a concert.

✪ Go window shopping.

✪ Go out to inspect some new home displays.

✪ Go to a nice hotel or motel for the night.

✪ Take a swim together

✪ Go hiking.

✪ Hire a limo.

✪ Go on a picnic.

✪ Walk on the beach.

✪ Fly a kite.

✪ Go on a cruise.

✪ Go to an amusement park.

✪ Cook breakfast out.

✪ Enjoy coffee and dessert out.

Those are just a few to get you going. Eagles enjoy life and have fun together. So should you.

Here are some secrets to say, "I love you".

♥ Just say it - often.

♥ Write it on the mirror with toothpaste.

♥ Write it on the calendar.

♥ Write it on a note under the pillow.

♥ Put an ad in the paper.

♥ Say it on the phone with a special call.

♥ Sing your partner a love song.

♥ Plant a tree to remind your partner of your love.

♥ Give flowers or a gift.

♥ Give your partner a rest by doing all the work in the home for a day.

♥ Write a card.

♥ Write a poem (if you are able).

♥ Plan a treasure hunt with a special prize at the end.

♥ Go on a moonlit walk.

♥ Send a letter saying, "I love you".

♥ Take the children out for a few hours.

Don't stop with these few - they are just starters.

Allow the eagles to teach us how to have a better, more enjoyable, marriage.

Living Like An Eagle

10. LIVING LIKE AN EAGLE

Courage

One of the main enemies of the young eagle is the serpent, especially in the tropics where snakes commonly inhabit the upper foliage of the rain forest where the eagle's nest is located. Here again, the eagle is unafraid of its adversary. Despite the fact that it has no immunity against the venom, it will present its breast as a target for the snake. Once the snake has struck and missed, the eagle retaliates with lightning speed, seizing the writhing serpent in its razor sharp talons. Sometimes the eagle will feint, allowing the snake to repeatedly strike. Once the vulnerable head is offguard, the bird pounces.

Usually the eagle will fly off to a nearby tree or rocky ledge where the body of the snake is systematically passed through the talons until the head is seized firmly, then the bird proceeds to decapitate it before carrying the writhing body back to the nest as food for the young. Courage is not the absence of fear; it is the mastery of it.

Success is never final and failure is never fatal; it is courage that counts.

Are you ready to run when the heat rises? About to quit? Every day, in some way, your courage will be tested.

Courage is a three letter word. Real courage is saying "yes" to life, not backing down when we face adversity. Courage is acting with fear, not without it.

"You gain strength, courage and confidence by every experience, but you must stop and look fear in the face...You must do the thing you think you cannot do."
[Eleanor Roosevelt]

Here are some suggestions to create courage:

1. Live for a great and high cause. What great dreams do you have that keep you awake at night?

2. Remember, people are counting on you. Your family, your organisation, your team.

3. Keep your dreams vividly before you at all times. Obstacles are what you see when you take your eyes off the goals.

THE ONLY WAY TO WIN

*It takes a little courage
And a little self-control,
And some grim determination,
If you want to reach your goal.
It takes a deal of striving
And a firm and stern-set chin,
No matter what the battle,
If you really want to win.*

*There's no easy path to glory,
There's no rosy road to fame.
Life, however we may view it
Is no simple parlour game;
But its prizes call for fighting,
For endurance and for grit;
For a rugged disposition
And a don't-know-when-to-quit.*

*You must take a blow or give one,
You must risk and you must lose,
And expect that in the struggle
You will suffer from the bruise.
But you must not wince or falter
If a fight you once begin;
Be a man and face the battle
That's the only way to win.*

Remember - Courage is not the absence of fear but the mastery of it.

Boldness

Eagles possess remarkable qualities - most of which we would be well advised to duplicate. One of the finest attributes the bird possesses is its boldness. In Russia and Mongolia where the eagle is used to hunt the wolf, the birds fear nothing. "Harpy" in Aztec means "winged wolf" and the Harpy Eagle is the most powerful eagle of all, standing three feet tall, weighing over 20 pounds and sporting a magnificent wing span of over 7 feet. The Harpy makes a formidable foe - its razor sharp talons allow it to hunt and kill animals three times its size and weight. Eagles dwell, live and even die on high, where few other birds nest. These magnificent birds are happy to dwell alone, not in colonies or bands as many other birds, but to stand alone against the world and the elements. The eagle rarely bows to pressure, succumbs to adversity...the eagle never begs bread!

The eagle never begs! In fact eagles are a breed apart, not easily discouraged. Whether it be in the heat of the Australian desert or the freezing winds of the North American continent rarely will the eagle leave or desert its nesting site or young. Many lesser birds flee the Winter storms, returning again with the Spring sunshine...not so the eagle.

If you want to achieve in life you will have to overcome your timidity. So many are afraid to speak to people. Here are a few suggestions to help you to step out in boldness.

1. Speak to people. There's nothing as nice as a cheerful greeting.

2. Smile at people. It takes 72 muscles to frown and only 14 to smile.

3. Call people by name. The sweetest music to the ears is one's own name.

4. Be friendly and helpful. If you would have friends, be friendly.

5. Be cordial. Speak and act as if everything you do is a pleasure.

6. Be genuinely interested in people.

7. Be generous with praise, cautious with criticism.

8. Be considerate with the feelings of others; it will be appreciated.

9. Be thoughtful of others' opinions. There are three sides to every controversy - yours, the other's and the right one.

10. Be alert to give service. What counts a great deal in life is what we do for others.

One of the things people fear most is public speaking. Here again are some keys to help you.

1) Know what you are going to say in advance.

2) Look your listeners in the eye.

3) Take your time. Talk clearly, concisely and deliberately.

4) Use an outline instead of memorising a speech.

5) Be constructive. Stress the merits of your viewpoint, not the flaws in someone else's.

6) Use visual aids to engage your audience's eyes as well as ears and capitalise by using gestures to emphasise important points.

7) Go beyond self-interest. Showing the audience how you can help them achieve what they want is much more effective than putting yourself in the limelight.

8) Be specific.

9) Be yourself. You can learn from others, but don't make the mistake of trying to imitate a successful orator.

10) Use a positive approach.

11) Stop at the right time. When you sense that you have scored your points and that the audience gets the message, stop talking.

Relentless Attacker

An eagle determined on attacking is a fearsome opponent. Few creatures attack with the relentless fury of an eagle protecting its family or domain.

Don't allow life to beat you.

Climb 'til your dream comes true

Often your tasks will be many and more than you think you can do.
Often the road will be rugged and the hills insurmountable too.
But always remember the hills ahead are never as steep as they seem,
And with faith in your heart start upward and climb 'til you reach your dream.
For nothing in life that is worthy is ever too hard to achieve
If you have the courage to try it and you have the faith to believe;
For faith is a force that is greater than knowledge or power or skill
And many defeats turn to triumph, if you determine to win you will.
So, climb 'til your dreams come true!

Hanging On

Eagles have the ability to clasp onto their prey with incredible power and force. Very few creatures escape once they fall into the clutches of an eagle's lethal talons. In fact, eagle trainers quickly discover that even in a roosting position (on a heavily padded arm) the bird can fire his razor sharp talons clean through several layers of leather and into the flesh, when aroused or excited. In many cases the talons actually lock so that they cannot even be prised loose but are released only by enticing the eagle with food.

Eagles swooping onto swimming fish strike with such devastating power that the talons may actually be forced clean through the fish protruding from the other side. Someone has calculated that eagles strike with the same amount of energy as that released from an elephant rifle. All eagles make use of their feet to kill, each foot comprises four toes, one behind and three forward, each armed with long deadly talons, the hind talon being particularly lethal and scimitar shaped.

Fish eating eagles have rough textured spicules which give them a better hold on their slippery prey, while others, such as the golden eagle, rely on their more deadly and powerful grip. Once the bird locks its powerful talons onto its prey, nothing - but nothing - will prise them loose. In fact so tight does it maintain a hold that fish have been washed ashore with the dead body of an eagle still attached, the deadly talons still firmly and powerfully embedded in its prey. The fish being too powerful or heavy for the bird, caused it to be dragged beneath the water to its death. But the bird would rather die than release its hold!

Courage, boldness, tenacity, just plain "grit" - this is the eagle.

Don't you dare give up or give in. "Hang in there, baby, you can do it."

Fight on to achieve your dreams and goals. It's always too soon to quit.

Fight like an eagle.

Renewal

11. RENEWAL

Probably the single most impressive quality of the eagle is the bird's remarkable ability to renew its youth.

There comes a time in the life of every eagle when it is somewhat slower in flight. Indeed the wing feathers begin to give off a tell-tale whistle as the bird dives at its prey. Often the whistle of the wings is enough to warn a rabbit or fish and it is able to dodge the attack. Besides problems with its feathers the eagle may also find its talons are blunt and calcifications have formed on its beak. Seemingly the king of the sky is ready for the old folk's home. Yet at this critical stage in the eagle's life it flies to the high country, up close to the sun.

High in the mountains the eagle proceeds to go through a remarkable process of rejuvenation. Firstly it starts to pluck at some of its wing feathers. One by one the faulty feathers are "cast off". Firstly it gets rid of the problem. One report had a particular variety of eagle stripping itself completely bald and awaiting some forty days for a complete regrowth of feathers.

Next the bird may seek out a cool refreshing mountain stream to wash itself. Eagles are very clean birds in their natural state. The icy waters remove the taint and stain of death, the lice and parasites, the old and dull feathers, the muck and filth of the world. Fresh, clean and naked, the eagle stands before the sun.

We too may experience times in our lives when we are dry, stale, depressed, weak or defeated. The world has dealt us a bitter blow, ruffled our feathers so to speak. We may have lost our confidence, had our dreams explode in our face.

HONING BY THE ROCK

While awaiting the regrowth of its flight feathers the eagle also does something about a dull beak - perhaps blunted by rocks or the growth of a calcium buildup. The beak is an all important weapon and must be kept lethally sharp. Like a soldier preparing his sword for battle the calcifications are painstakingly ground away by the slow but steady action of the beak against the rock. Likewise the talons too may be sharpened or removed altogether. Relentlessly the beak and talons are methodically honed back to lethal sharpness, ready for the world.

Soon we too like the eagle are transformed. The defeated, negative patterns, ideas and thoughts are removed. Eventually after many days of preening, plucking, honing, grinding and washing, the eagle is ready to return to the outside world. He spreads his huge wings and alights from the mountain peaks a new bird. Its youth has been renewed. Again it is a powerful, dangerous bird to contend with. A bird to strike fear into the heart of every serpent. The king of the sky moves off to survey his domain with new feathers for soaring, new beak for slashing and a new set of talons for grasping prey. He soars aloft rolling, swooping, turning and diving at the earth at incredible speeds of 100 kph. A bird with new life, new strength and a new joy for living!

Perhaps there is a need in your life to repair the dream. Maybe you have hit a ceiling or levelled out on a plateau. It's time to get renewed.
Have you lost the enthusiasm and the motivation?

Here are some ways to get it restored so you can soar through the clouds again.

1. Keep reading good motivational books.

2. Keep on listening to motivational tapes.

3. Keep on mixing with motivational people.

4. Read inspirational biographies.

5. Look to good mentors.

6. Keep physically fit.

7. Eat the right food.

8. Don't be depleted for rest and relaxation. Keep your reservoirs full.

9. Make lists.

10. Take action. Do it now.

11. Take advantage of energy peaks.

12. Be optimistic.

13. Work on your character.

14. Live life enthusiastically.

15. Invest in yourself.

16. Take a vacation. Fatigue makes cowards of us all.

17. Re-evaluate your goals.

18. Keep developing your skills.

19. Think positively.

20. Encourage others.

21. Write out your visions and dreams again.

Spend some time to get re-created. If you don't come apart, you may well come apart!

Get refreshed for your own sake, your family's, friends' and your team's.

Spend some time to renew yourself. Again you will soar like the eagle you are with new life, new strength and a new joy for living.

Fly up to the high country. Get yourself renewed. Re-sharpen your skills and presentation. Attack life better than ever.

Attack life like an eagle.

Chapter

12

Come Fly

12. COME FLY

An American Indian tells about a brave who found an eagle's egg and put it into the nest of a prairie chicken. The eaglet hatched with the brood of chicks and grew up with them.

All his life the changeling eagle, thinking he was a prairie chicken, did what the prairie chickens did. He scratched in the dirt for seeds and insects to eat. He clucked and cackled. And he flew in a brief thrashing of wings and flurry of feathers no more than a few feet off the ground. After all, that's how prairie chickens are supposed to fly.

Years passed. And the changeling eagle grew very old. One day he saw a magnificent bird far above him in the cloudless sky. Hanging with graceful majesty on the powerful wind currents, it soared with scarcely a beat of its strong golden wings.

"What a beautiful bird!" said the changeling eagle to his neighbour, "What is it?"

"That's an eagle - the chief of the birds," the neighbour clucked, "but don't give it a second thought. You could never be like him."

So the changeling eagle never gave it another thought.

And it died thinking it was a prairie chicken.

What a tragedy. Built to soar into the heavens, but conditioned to stay earthbound, that eagle pecked at stray seeds and chased insects. Though designed to be among the most awesome of all fowl, he instead believed his neighbour's counsel: "Hey, you're only a prairie chicken...Come on, let's go find us some insects."

No. You are designed to fly. Your full potential is waiting. Life, with all its excitement, is ready to be seized.

My friend, Darin Browne, expressed it beautifully in his song, "Eagles' Wings":-

I spent my days looking at the ground
I thought the world had clipped my wings
I spent the hours saying I felt down
I had no strength. I felt entangled in things

And then I hear You call me
Set my face into the breeze
I lift my head. I spread my wings and I am free

My heart was heavy in the valley down below
My soul was empty, void of love
My sight was clouded by the dust the world did blow
I set my mind on earth not things above.

But now your Spirit lifts me
From the dust in which I lie
I will not be conquered. I am destined for the sky

CHORUS

Let me fly, let me fly
On the eagle wings on high
Let me rise above what I never have before
Lift me up to the sky
Let me lift my voice and cry
Let me fly and sing
Stretch forth my Eagles' wings
[Darin Browne] - used by permission

It's time to give up your small ambitions. It's time to take
a leap like the eagle, to stretch those wings, to rise above
the mountains, through the clouds.

TO SOAR WITH THE EAGLES

What is the key? BELIEF.

It is not possible for human beings to be empty vessels. No one who has ever lived has been an unbeliever, despite what he or she may argue. Everyone believes in something. It might be God or no God, wealth or poverty, power or weakness, winning or losing. It might be a belief in a career or a friend, in science or a principle. But everyone believes in something. Show me what you are committed to and I will tell you who you are. Whatever it is that we place before ourselves is what we will move toward.

You can fly. Believe it. You can do it.

It's time to soar with the eagles.

ENDNOTES

I am so grateful to all those who have helped me in getting resource material on eagles. People like our Australian farmers ("we call them 'cockeys'!")

Ideas came from World Book Encyclopaedia, Volume E; Character sketches from the Institute in Basic Youth Conflicts, Volume III; "On Eagles' Wings" by Col Stringer.

Especially I would like to thank my friend Darin Browne of Servant's Heart Ministries for the words from "Eagles' Wings".

BEST SELLING BOOKS BY BILL NEWMAN:

1. THE TEN LAWS OF LEADERSHIP

Just as there are principles that govern nature, so there are definite principles which are vital in leadership. Don't stagger on in ignorance. Study well these principles to become the leader you are meant to be.

2. THE POWER OF A SUCCESSFUL LIFE

No one wants to climb the ladder of success only to find the the ladder is leaning against the wrong wall! Success is a series of right choices. Here are the exciting keys to success - principles that have proven so effective in the lives of so many - just waiting to be proven in yours.

3. HOW TO CONQUER WORRY

Is there a cure for care and worry? (termed the 'official emotion of our age' and 'the world's greatest modern plague') 10 golden keys teaching us how to conquer and overcome worry through the Great Physician.

4. FAMILY LIFE IN THE FAST LANE

The needs of families have never been greater than today. Bill Newman gives you some sensible keys for strengthening and enriching marriage and family life.

Return to
**Bill Newman International
PO Box 195
TOOWONG QLD 4066
Australia**

BOOK ORDER FORM

		QTY	$.00

1. THE TEN LAWS OF LEADERSHIP $12.00 _____ _____

2. THE POWER OF A SUCCESSFUL LIFE $10.00 _____ _____

3. HOW TO CONQUER WORRY $10.00 _____ _____

4. FAMILY LIFE IN THE FAST LANE $10.00 _____ _____

5. SOARING WITH EAGLES (extra copies) $10.00 _____ _____

Post/Packing: Orders under $20 add $2.50;
 $20-$50 add $5.00; over $50 - P.O.A.   _____ _____
Payable to Bill Newman International

TOTAL   ====== =====

Name
....
Address
....

....

Ph. ....P/C...

Return to BILL NEWMAN INTERNATIONAL
PO Box 195 TOOWONG QLD 4066 AUSTRALIA